Our children shall serve the Lord
and tell future generations about Him.

Psalm 22:30

To Charles-Edward, Israel, and Faith
(For keeping me on track with a trillion questions!)

Text Copyright © 2025 by Nancy Owusu Adu
Illustrations Copyright © 2025 by Christina Rudenko

Verses marked WEB are taken from the World English Bible. All rights reserved. No part of this work may be reproduced or transmitted in any form or by any means, electronic or mechanical including, photocopying, or by any information storage or retrieval system, except as is explicitly permitted by the Copyright Act or in writing from the author.

ISBN: 979-8-9922853-0-7 - Paperback
ISBN: 979-8-9922853-1-4 - Hardcover

NBeirene Press

MY BODY IS IN THE BIBLE!
Bring the Scriptures to life for your toddler

By Nancy Owusu Adu　　　　　　Illustrated by Christina Rudenko

God makes me strong! He shows my hands and fingers how to fight.

Psalm 144:1

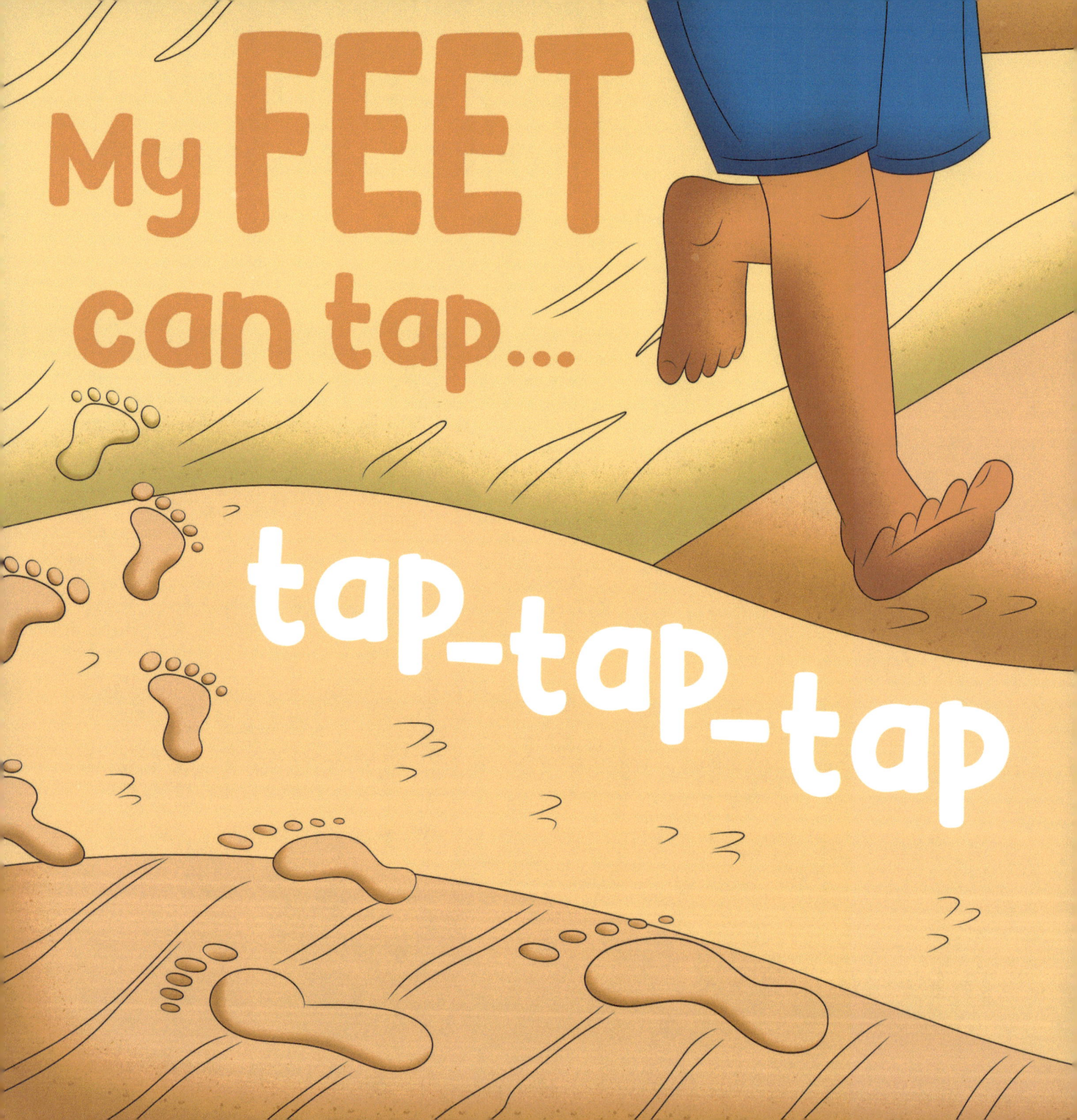

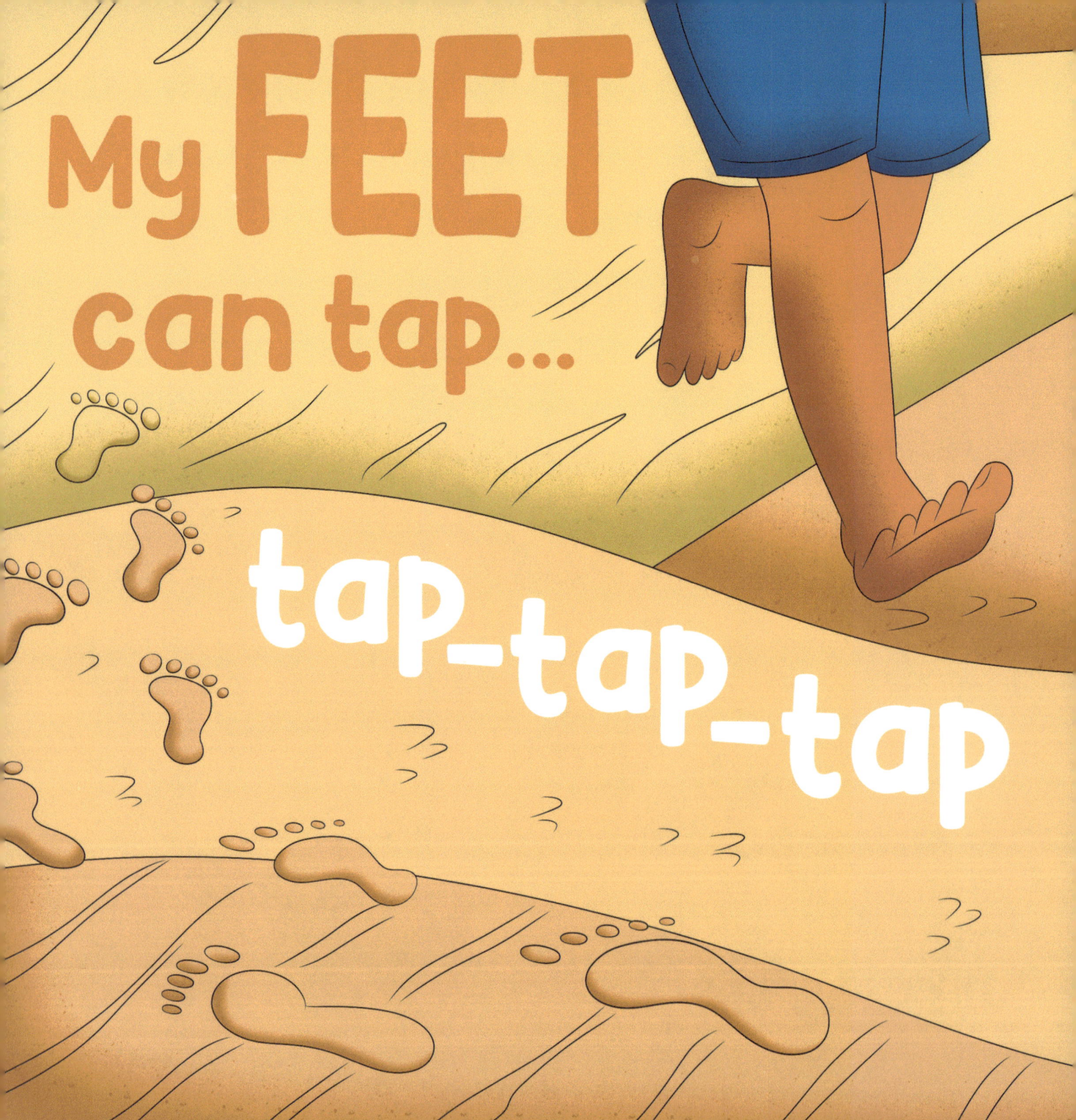

Everything in your word is beautiful. Open my eyes to see them all!

Psalm 119:18

God will rescue my feet from every trap. I will always keep my eyes on Him.

Psalm 25:15

My MOUTH can count God's blessings

My mouth shall be filled with your praise, with your honor all the day.

Psalm 71:8 WEB

Your words are better than honey and taste sweet in my mouth.

Psalm 119:103

I am special! You even know the exact number of hair on my head! I have nothing to be afraid of!!

Luke 12:7

You bless me by pouring oil on my head. I have more than enough.

Psalm 23:5b

I clap my hands and praise God with a shout!!!
Psalm 47:1

God makes my hands strong for war, my arms can break a bow.
2 Samuel 22:35

Sacrifices are not what makes you happy, listening to you with my ears does.

Psalm 40:6

When I turn to the right or to the left, my ears can hear a voice behind me telling me the right way to go.

Isaiah 30:21

Everything you have said is true, my tongue sings about them all.
Psalm 119:172

I speak beautiful things about my King. My tongue is like a writer's pen!
Psalm 45:1

My whole BODY can praise God!

I will give thanks to you for I am fearfully and wonderfully made.

Psalm 139 14 WEB

A Word from the Author

It has been a great joy of mine seeing this book become a reality!

Your opinion matters to me! If you enjoyed reading this book, I would greatly appreciate it if you could take a few minutes to leave a review on Amazon. Your kind feedback is appreciated and inspires me to keep doing more.
Thank you!

www.ingramcontent.com/pod-product-compliance
Lightning Source LLC
Chambersburg PA
CBHW041135130526
44582CB00031B/135